The Teacher as Evangelist (Revised)

by
Irene Smith Caldwell

**Preface and Guidance
for Effective Use
by Arlo F. Newell**

Published by
Warner Press, Inc.
Anderson, Indiana

Table of Contents

Preface

Successful Christian education always eventuates in successful evangelism . . . confronting all persons with the "good news" that they might respond to God's redeeming love as revealed in Christ. I was always impressed with the late Irene Caldwell's concern about giving persons an opportunity to make a decision to serve Christ, to respond in love and obedience to God's will. The conversion of persons to Christ had long been the concern of her life. This response though is more than just a decision, it is the beginning of a continuing, growing experience in Christ.

In a very real way the response is the result of a team effort within the church. Paul spoke of this when he said: "I have planted, Apollos watered; but God gave the increase." (1 Cor. 3:6). The pastor, church school teachers, parents, curriculum writers, class members have all shared in helping to lead someone personally to accept Jesus Christ as Savior. This response may come at the end of a class session, during the devotions of the class, or even during a social gathering in someone's home, but it is the result of all working together to accomplish our task of evangelizing the world.

This book is a tool to be used in a multipurpose ministry. Parents seeking to better understand their growing children will find it helpful for exploring their developmental stages in physical growth and spiritual understanding. Church school teachers who desire methods, scripture verses and other helps will find it a guide pointing the way to an implementation of evangelism at every level. The busy pastor who wants a concise presentation for parent/teacher groups will find it extremely helpful in discussing Christian education as an open door for leading persons to conversion through Christ. The Board of Christian Education in every local church should study it thoroughly for ideas which they might adapt for their particular program of soul winning in their community. No one program is adequate in totality for every church. For that reason it is important for the Board of Christian Education to study a variety of methods from which to adapt an approach which will produce greatest results in your given areas of ministry.

Personal soul winning is a shared responsibility. We are responsible for making salvation known to the world in which we live, therefore we would do well to share with one another the progress made in leading another to respond to God's love. The church school teacher needs to maintain a close tie with the parents, informing them of the progress of the pupil as the Holy Spirit deals with his or her life. Even such things as a response to particular passages of scripture, to the presentation of the lesson, or a reaction to particular social needs or church activities can be very important in enabling that pupil to commit his or her life to Christ. Caution should be exercised in sharing, guarding against breaking any particular confidence placed in you by the pupil. As the teacher shares with the parent, so the parent should openly share with the teacher about avenues of soul winning to which the pupil is receptive. Particular needs or experiences of the pupil shared with the teacher enables him or her to plan lessons or activities applicable to the needs of the individual. This makes the evangelical witness of the church more meaningful to the life situation of those we seek to lead to salvation. It is always wise to begin at the point of one's greatest need and that can only be known and understood when we share together as co-workers in personal soul winning.

—Arlo F. Newell

CHAPTER 1

That They May Respond to Faith and Love

Have you stood on the beach and watched children building a castle in the sand? Just as they are about to finish the castle, they notice that each swell of the ocean brings the water closer. They quickly throw up a protective dike. That failing, they surround the castle with their own bodies to try to protect it. But soon the swelling tide has leveled the castle. Nearby craggy rocks resist the tide and remain the same regardless of the changes in the tide, or the storminess of the ocean.

The sand castle and the craggy rock, it seems to me, symbolize much that is happening in the church's thinking about evangelism. Tides change unnoticed, and the church goes on trying to use the same ingrained practices, even defending them with all their strength, unmindful of swirling currents of the world within which they must operate. But in spite of the currents of change, some things are steadfast.

WHAT THINGS ARE STEADFAST?

The good news of redemption through Christ will never change. The hunger for this good news is in the heart of persons in all times and cultures. *The need to make the gospel known* is timeless. In fact, evangelism is the business of the church.

Evangelism is inherent in Christian education for education is not Christian unless the aim is to "so make known the good news of redemption through Christ that persons of all ages will respond to God's love in trust and obedience." Evangelism, then has three components: (1) There is the responsibility on the part of Christians to help all persons to become sensitive to God's love for them and his continuous call; (2) there is the challenge to make a clear and definite response, and (3) there is guidance in how to be disciples and how to mature in the Christian life. No part of this comprehensive conception of evangelism may be neglected in the church's work of Christian education.

The aim which has become basic to the church's curriculum clearly expresses these three purposes: that all persons become aware of God through all the ways he makes himself known, especially through his redeeming love as revealed in Christ Jesus, and that they respond in faith and love—to the end that as new persons in Christ they may know who they are and what their human situation means, grow as children of God rooted in the Christian community, yield themselves to the Holy Spirit, live in obedience to the will of God in every relationship, fulfill their common discipleship and mission in the world and abide in the Christian hope.

WHAT IS EVANGELISM?

Here capsulized in one statement is a comprehensive interpretation of evangelism. God is confronting persons in many ways, but primarily through love as revealed in Christ Jesus. Through responding in faith and love persons become new creatures, then growth takes place as they continually yield themselves to the Holy Spirit, and live in obedience to God in every relationship. The whole purpose of Christian education is to make this possible for all persons. However, in the experience of the church, the idea of evangelism has sometimes been given a more limited meaning: to indicate intensive short-term efforts to win persons to make decisions for Christ, or to confront persons personally for such a decision. Such an approach assumes that the teaching ministry is something apart from evangelism.

In actual practice, unfortunately, there is often a separation in the minds of some. The church school may engage its members in Bible study, social activities, and service projects with little expectation that these experiences will lead to a personal response to God's love and commitment to His will. But is it not time that all the church does must be with the expectation that the "good news of God's love and forgiveness" will be communicated both within the church and in the world? The expectation is that persons will "respond in faith and love" through their experiences in the church school. They need not wait for a special "evangelistic" emphasis.

As we deal with evangelism and Christian education, we will think first of this broader interpretation. This will emphasize the guidance of each person so as to prepare the way for continuing response to God's confrontation at every period in life. For children this will mean laying foundations of trust which may develop into faith. For youth it may mean the challenge to live by high values regardless of the cost. For adults it may be a growing understanding and commitment to responsible decision-making. Evangelism in this sense is a spirit of concern for growth toward Christian maturity. Such a spirit must permeate the whole of Christian education.

But evangelism also means bringing all persons to a personal experience with Christ as Savior and Lord. Such a goal cannot be separated from the broader goal of evangelism. In truth, they are both a part of the whole pattern. Teaching which does not lead to conversion and continued confrontation and growth is not Christian; but conversion without nurture is likely to be temporary or sub-Christian.

Evangelism, therefore, cannot be programmed. It cannot be identified with any particular method or procedure. No one of us can presume to say how God may speak to another. To some persons conversion comes as a great leap forward—a clear and identifiable experience accompanied by unforgettable emotion. They know themselves to have been touched by God, forgiven and in fellowship with Him.

To others, the experience seems to come into focus more gradually. They may have been responding to God's love from childhood. But even they will make a definite decision, an act of commitment of life to God.

The Bible describes the change that comes through such a definite commitment as "being born again," "left all to follow Christ," "passing from darkness to light," "being born of the spirit." The church must always be aware that the pupil's response to God's confrontation is a high point of its teaching ministry.

This booklet is intended to alert leaders to opportunities for evangelism in the teaching-learning experiences of the church. It is based on the assumption that evangelism is inherent in the educational ministry of the church. The focus is on helping leaders to be sensitive to the level of the learner's commitment, a readiness to respond to Christ as Savior and Lord, and to answer to the demands that commitment makes upon one's life.

Evangelism is the great mission of the church, but it needs to be understood in a broad sense, which incorporates laying foundations, conversions and maturing in obedience and commitment.

CHAPTER II

For Everything
There Is a Season

The writer of the sayings of Ecclesiastes had a keen sense of timing when he said, "For everything there is a season, and a time for every matter under heaven" (Eccl. 3:1 RSV). So, as we think of evangelism, we realize that the emphasis will differ in varying periods of life. While one's response to God is a very personal thing, there are seasons for planting, seasons for growth, and seasons for the ripening of the spirit. What, then, is evangelism at the differing periods of life?

A CHILD IS BORN
(BIRTH TO 3 YEARS)

"The human being is the most unfinished of creatures at the time of his birth," so Wayne Oates begins his chapter on "Faith as the Source of Human Personality." He continues to say that parents are "invited, urged, and required as co-laborers with God to join in finishing his new creation."[1]

In Christian education today there are two languages of teaching: the language of relationships and the language of words, and the language of relationships must be experienced before words can have meaning. Long before the child can use language he can feel love and trust. Young children can experience the reality of God though in a non-verbal way. Such an experience seems to include at least wonder, joy, love and trust. These are very akin to worship. So evangelism for the very young child means laying firm emotional foundations which may grow into faith.

Since the first three years of a person's life are now known to be significantly related to later attitudes toward life and religion, the church is realizing the qualifications necessary for leadership in the nursery classes. Let no nursery teacher feel that she or he is not an evangelist. If trust is to be the very foundation for response, then here is a great opportunity. What, then, are characteristics essential for the nursery?

1. Trust is based on consistency. Young children should be cared for by the same core of workers Sunday after Sunday. How can they grow in trust if they meet different persons and different treatment each Sunday? How can they learn to respond in love? Do we want children to reach out in expressions of love and trust to every adult, or are these to be growing, earned responses?

2. Love is expressed through care. Children learn love for those who care for their physical needs, if such care is accompanied by cuddling and other tender physical contacts.

3. Theological foundations are laid. Teachers of young children need a sound theology. Of course they will not use theology terms, but their concepts of a loving, forgiving and victorious God come through to children on the feeling level. In truth, the nursery is the place for sensitive, mature and experienced Christians, who have a joyous faith and who love God and children.

As the child begins to understand and use words, we will foster in the child a love for Jesus, who came as a baby and grew to be a person who loved children and helped the sick and hungry. The children will come to think of Jesus as a special person sent by God, and the Bible as the book that tells about him and they will feel love for Jesus and desire to be like him. They will think of God as one who made them and gives them so many happy and beautiful things. But chiefly, they will learn through sensing that the church is a place where they are loved and warmly accepted.

THE KINDERGARTEN YEARS (4 AND 5 YEARS)

During the kindergarten years children should feel a growing love for Jesus. They will come to form clearer ideas of Jesus' life on earth, and know that he came to show God's great love. Since these children are literal minded, avoid abstract and symbolic terms and religious ideas beyond their experiences.

They can become real friends of Jesus and desire to do only that which would please him.

They can have true experiences of worship, and pray for strength to do right. They can find forgiveness if they feel they have done wrong, and they can have experiences of forgiving others.

Care needs to be taken that the child's experience is genuine rather than an artificial form or ritual following adult practices. The sensitivity of children makes them responsive to emotional appeals or adult pressures, even though they may not understand meanings or be able to follow out the implications of the response. Not every "religious" experience is wholesome for the child. If responses do not grow out of the child's own understanding or experiences, they are not authentic. Teachers are often satisfied to hear children "mouth" words without real meaning to them. They may give what have been dubbed as "Sunday school answers," Such as:

Teacher: What does Jesus want us to do?
Children: Be good
Teacher: What else?
Children: Obey our parents
Teacher: Are there other things?
Children: Pray and come to Sunday school.

Children may even go through the form of repentance without real feelings or understanding. The difference is much like the difference between a Christmas tree and an apple tree. The Christmas tree may look beautiful but the ornaments are put there from the outside, while the fruit hanging on the apple tree is of the very essence of the tree itself.

There is a danger, if we press experiences too early, that we may make young pharisees who can go through the form, but have not experienced the reality. Authenticity is the very core of genuine religion. Fear and form grow into doubt; trust and acceptance grow into faith.

THE PRIMARY AND MIDDLE YEARS (GRADES 1-4)

Children during these years are very different in their emotional development. Studies seem to indicate that children who have been carefully nurtured in home and church develop readiness for the definite conversion experience earlier than those who have not had such care.

"Sometimes I don't like myself very well" was the open confession of a six-year-old boy to his teacher friend. It was a summer evening and they had gone to the lake and were watching the sunset from a boat. The moment of worship and fellowship had brought the boy to a realization that something was wrong. Even he felt, to put it in his own words, that "sometimes I'm not very good." Such experiences should be used to help the child to a more meaningful relationship to God. The teacher might say, "Sometimes I feel that way, too, and then I pray and tell Jesus that I'm sorry. Then I know that he still loves me and will help me do better." The teacher might even help the child to express that desire through prayer, and usually the child will find quick relief and joy. These children are not yet ready for mature theological concepts. We will simply explain that Jesus, God's son, came to show us what God is like and to help us love God and one another. The emphasis will be on the fact that the Bible tells us that Jesus still lives and is a friend and helper for them today.

We will endeavor to develop a real love for Jesus and the church, and a desire to do what the Bible teaches. In doing so we lay firm foundations for acceptance of Jesus Christ as personal Savior and Lord.

THE PRE-ADOLESCENT YEARS (AGES 9-12)

The years from nine to twelve are often years of quickened religious consciousness. The junior should begin to see Jesus' life as a complete and connected whole; the junior can understand something of Jesus' divine nature and mission. He or she is now to the point of making significant decisions in many areas of life. The junior's consciousness takes in symbolic and abstract ideas. Pre-adolescence is usually a stable emotional part of life, therefore, it seems to be the "season" when a definite commitment to Christ can become vital.

Since each person is a free being, salvation is not arbitrarily imposed on them either by God or by teachers. The experience involves response on the part of the person. God freely offers salvation in steadfast love, but each individual person, must make a decision. As they come to understand God's love for them, many pre-adolescents will be ready to respond to His love and commit their lives to Christ as their Savior and Lord. Their experiences may have more emphasis on *decision for* Christ and *desire to follow* the Christian life, than on *turning around* or *turning away* from sin. Yet even these children may feel a need for asking forgiveness and finding renewed fellowship with God and the church. If during revival services or other church experiences young children go to the altar, teachers who understand them should counsel and pray with them. Such an experience can be a genuine forward move for the child if he or she is responding to an inner desire to follow Christ. The response must be followed up with personal care and guidance in order that every response develops into a wholesome pattern of spiritutal growth. Some, however, may not have reached the maturity where this important decision can be made with understanding. Whether or not this high point of decision—the conversion experience—is reached now, each person should make steady growth in the desire and determination to live as a follower of Jesus Christ.

THE TEEN YEARS

The age of thirteen has a sort of magic in the minds of youth. The thirteen-year-old has joined the teen-age society and no longer thinks of himself or herself as a child (even though parents and teachers often treat the thirteen-year-old as a child). This is a particularly ripe season for religious development. Gordon Allport says that "to feel oneself meaningfully linked to the whole of Being is not possible before puberty." He describes the adolescent as one "whose passion for integrity and for meaningful relationships to the whole of Being is his most distinctive capacity."[2]

This is not to say that until this time of definite freely-chosen decision there has been no relationship to Christ. Indeed the young teen has been one of Christ's "little ones." He or she may have prayed and had true communion with God as well as asked and received God's forgiveness when feeling guilty. He or she may even have had an altar decision experience. But until the young teen becomes a responsible, self-determining person, religion may have been largely the result of environment and the choice of parents. He or she has been responding in the expected way of the community of faith. Hopefully, those experiences have been so rich and meaningful that now the young person may "respond in faith and love" of the individual's very own choice.

It is impossible to predict when a youth may have developed to this stage of decision. Parents and teachers will be sensitive to such development and will keep the door open for the response. They will remember that there are varieties of conversion experiences, even for this age.

If as a child the youth has developed a desire to follow Christ, this relationship will deepen as he or she becomes more free to make a personal decision. Then we will challenge each youth to make a decisive choice for God and the Christian way of life.

There are two dangers that are to be avoided at this sensitive period. One is that the young person may grow up thinking of himself or herself as a Christian and never realize the true experience of conversion. The individual has never taken the definite, volitional step of accepting Jesus Christ as Savior and Lord. Therefore, the Christian experience is second-hand and powerless. If teachers have built a relationship with the youth, they can explore an individual relationship with God. Even if the young person feels definite about the experience, such a conversation may affirm the decision and "give direction" to the teachers as they sponsor the maturing process.

The other danger is that teachers may violate the personality by pressing beyond the individual's own choice. God is ever seeking all persons with redemptive love, but if the person refuses, salvation cannot come. Youth can learn that they become responsible for their own choices. They can understand that God does not make his children commit their ways unto him. He helps them, and they can avail themselves of that help to the extent that they desire it. The teacher's part, then, is to help persons recognize their need of God and to help them experience his love so that they may respond to his confrontation with answering love, trust and obedience.

Who are we to say at what age such an authentic experience of conversion may take place! Some children seem more spiritually sensitive than others. Many children do have genuine crises experiences at an early age. This decision may have been sincere and appropriate for the time and age. No person is a static being; but always growing, changing, becoming. With the often turbulent change from childhood to adolescence, the young person may feel almost like a different individual. Those childhood experiences may seem unreal and far away. Decisions made earlier seem hardly one's own for the person has changed so greatly.

Most youth seem to feel the need for either a crises-type decision or for an affirming one during adolescence, regardless of earlier religious experiences. "Now that I have become a person on my own," as one youth expressed it, "I want to rethink my Christian decision and get this thing settled once and for all."

CHAPTER III

Seasons In Adulthood

Once I experienced a devastating forest fire in the High Sierras of California. For days the fire roared through the giant Sequoias bringing death and destruction. The sky was red from the blaze. Finally the fire was overcome by a drenching rain. Stark, charred poles reached into the sky. The fire was under control, but as we drove down from the mountaintop I saw smoldering, smoking coals deep down in the roots of many of the larger trees.

To me this is a parable of the Christian life. (Remember a parable is told to make clear one major point.) Through conversion the victory has been won; the direction of life has been set, but deep down in the recesses of the mind un-Christian attitudes may still be smoldering. The struggle may still be going on, sometimes almost unconsciously, in areas of the will. New insights and challenges renew the struggle.

Even though as a child or youth a person may have made a definite decision for Christ and have been genuinely converted, nothing is settled "once and for all" except possibly the direction life will take. Each stage even of adulthood, has its own need of evangelism. Every adult, even though a Christian, has large areas of life that have yet to be evangelized. In fact, evangelism as we are defining it in this chapter, is a life-long process of confrontation and response.

We are deeply concerned, also, about winning those who have not accepted Christ as their Savior previously. Indeed, the church must find a way at every stage of life of initiating persons into a relationship with God through Christ. Some ways of reaching these people for Christ will be discussed in Chapter V.

Adulthood too has "seasons of the soul." Even those who earlier have responded to God's call have spiritual tasks to accomplish.

THE YOUNG ADULT

For the young adult the challenge is to change from a receiving person to a giving person. Now the task is to take a full share of responsibility emotionally, economically, socially and religiously. The greatest temptation is to remain uninvolved. The individual may choose to accept passively all benefits offered, but be unwilling to carry his or her part of the load.

The person's greatest need is to be able to give and receive mature love. Young adulthood is a fruitful season of the soul. Life choices are being made and directions are being set. The young adult is asking, "What will be the meaning of my life?" While evaluating the past the person tries to draw out that which is seen to have value. He or she wants to know fulfillment. But there are conflicting calls from many directions. There is the call to materialistic success; the call to selfish pleasure; the call to security. Could not the call to a life of adventure in the spirit be a greater challenge? But many young adults will never understand this possibility unless we, through our own spiritual vitality and victory hold before them a clear image of the true meaning of life.

THE MIDDLE ADULT

For the middle adult the challenge is to find the deeper meanings of life. The individual must find a spiritual base for coping with life. The greatest temptation is to seek for security in *things,* and thus base life on shifting materialistic values. The middle adult has the task of adjusting early dreams to reality. Often a sinking feeling of failure and even of guilt occurs. He or she sometimes feels a real discrepancy between the idealized life and the real life. The quest to bring integrity between "who I would like to be" and "who I feel I am" is one of the ripest fields for deep spiritual growth.

A mother said, "My children say I'm a hypocrite; that wouldn't bother me so much, except I'm afraid that I am. At least I don't have all the faith and victory others testify about. I've tried my very best, and I believe I'm a Christian but I'm often weak and discouraged with myself." Here is a suffering person who needs support in working through to self understanding and spiritual depths.

When the middle adult faces unanticipated reality, he or she may plumb a spiritual depth which hitherto had never been known. If death comes in the family; if loved ones refuse to accept Christ; if the person is forced or called to make a vocational change; if health fails, there are alternatives. They include: blaming others or even God; shutting out the reality; or using adversity to find God as he really is. Here is an opportunity for evangelism for Christ only can bring meaning and satisfaction to a life filled with drudgery when one has expected excitement, or with tragedy, sharp and bitter, or with a loneliness increased by the feeling that nobody cares. Every crises in life may become a call to deeper meaning and to a closer relationship with God.

THE OLDER ADULT

For the older adult the challenge is to maintain dignity and to find eternal value and meaning. The older adult needs to understand that God planned all of life; a season to be young, a season of middle adulthood, and a season to be elderly. Each season has its purpose and its particular challenge.

In a society that is youth, beauty, and work oriented, it may be difficult for the older adult to keep a clear sense of worth. Lewis Sherrill in his book *The Struggle of the Soul,* says that the older adult must distinguish the more important from the less important, and lay aside all hindrances. He says the task of the final stage is "achieving simplification of life in its physical, material and spiritual aspects, so that the soul may with less and less impediment progress toward its chosen destiny."[3]

The church must help people realize that all of life can be an upward path. The writer of Proverbs describes life in this way: "But the path of the just is as the shining light, that shineth more and more unto the perfect day" (Proverbs 4:18). How is worth to be judged? Is it by how much a person can produce? Is it by material possessions? Is it by physical strength and vigor? Or is it by the quality of the inner life? Numerous studies have shown a direct relationship between good personal adjustment in old age and participation in religious activities.[4] In times of stress and despair, religion provides meaning and comfort to those who in faith respond to its teaching. Most studies show that there is a greater interest in religion among older adults than at any other period of adulthood. As the end of life approaches, people find religion most helpful, and expressions of interest in religion becomes more common.[5] Older adults need the church and are open for evangelism. Even more than they need the church, the church needs them.

"We are often troubled, but not crushed; sometimes in doubt, but never in despair; there are many enemies but we are never without a friend; and though badly hurt at times, we are not destroyed" (2 Cor. 4:8-9 TEV). As they pare off nonessentials they come to the core of meaning, a steadfast relationship with God, and a simple love for others.

Evangelism, then, is not only leading persons to an experience, it is supporting them in the journey through life. Evangelism is helping persons find the deepest meanings in each period of life, from birth to death. Such meanings are grounded in the faith that humanity is created to live in relationship with God, and that there is a quality of wholeness about a life. Such Christian faith holds that all human experiences can become means of response to Christ and a growing relationship with him.

CHAPTER IV

Teaching
For Decision

"To be human is to be called on to make decisions. Therein lies the pain and splendor of being a person."[6]

It becomes the responsible privilege of the teacher to participate with pupils as they make basic value commitments. At the heart of such basic commitments is the decision to walk daily in the light as God shines it on his path. The song writer expressed it thusly:

> How beautiful to walk in the
>   steps of the Saviour
> Stepping in the light, stepping in
>   the light;
> How beautiful to walk in the
>   steps of the Saviour
> Led in paths of light.[7]

To teach for decision requires a new sense of your role as a teacher. It brings an aliveness to your life and your ministry. A teacher's version of Romans 12:11 might read

Never give in to tiredness, but serve the Lord with zest. Keep an aliveness in your class. Hold steady when trouble comes and just keep pray-

ing. Be warm and openhearted, and keep the cookie jar full.

Such a sense of aliveness comes from feeling that what you are doing is eternal. Your pupils may never become Christians if you fail to provide the challenge for them to make the decision.

Such a spirit of concern for bringing all persons to a relationship with Christ must permeate the whole of Christian education. This concern will express itself in many areas of decision. By this I mean that every lesson will have its "crossing point" with some life issue. In the experience, the Bible truth will be so related to some vital problem that persons will have to deal with the truth, and decide what to do about it in their own attitudes or actions. Harold Johnson calls this "Between Two Fires." He says

On one side
   the ache, the thrust, the yearning
      for survival with worth.
   On the other
   the promise fulfilled
      by God in Jesus Christ

   Between them is = (the equal sign)
      the daring act
      the church engaged
      in resolving the equation—
      the church teaching and learning.[8]

The = sign or maybe a + sign, is the teacher (the

evangelist) bringing together the need of the pupil and the promise fulfilled in Jesus Christ. The "crossing point" idea is that through teaching God calls to each person and shows the direction that person is to go. For example, the lesson for youth is on Amos the prophet, using the scripture, "But let justice roll down like waters and righteousness like an everflowing stream" (Amos 5:24 RSV). The real lesson will be to identify injustice, in their life situation, and help them to find ways to create justice. The truth of the scripture is to "cross over" into definite situations and call for decision in action.

Or an adult class is studying Ephesians and they come to the scripture, "Get rid of all bitterness, passion and anger. No more shouting, and insults! No more hateful feelings of any sort. Instead, be kind and tenderhearted to one another, and forgive one another as God has forgiven you in Christ (Eph. 4:31, 32 TEV). They talked about the scripture awhile, but they came to the crossing point when one member said, "When are we supposed to start practicing this? I came to the class so angry I couldn't think." Another said, "And what if it's Christians who treat you unjustly?" Another said, "And how do you get rid of hateful feelings?" At the end of the class one said, "I have some forgiving to do," and another said, "I'm afraid I must have a talk with my brother." This is teaching for decision.

Teaching can never be merely talking about

the Bible, nor even discussing about how to become a Christian. Rather, Christian teaching is helping persons made choices of great significance. Sometimes these choices will relate to choosing Christian values such as honesty, justice, respect for personality, or reverence. At other times the person will be confronted with the good news of God's love in Christ and will need to make a response.

Since such a response must be by the free choice of and distinctive to each learner, certain criteria may contribute to the genuineness of the experience.

1. The teacher should *be aware of class opportunities.*

In the elementary Sunday school curriculum there is a study about the life, death and resurrection of Jesus. Usually the lessons are prepared to provide for a challenge for persons to decide for Christ during the class. There are times when the spirit seems to move, and the sensitive teacher will provide the opportunity for the decision for Christ right there. The teacher may say, "We have heard the wonderful story of Jesus' birth and life. Recently we have been thinking about his death on the cross, and about his resurrection. He has shown us how much God loves us and wants us to love him.

"Of course we love him, but there comes a time when each person must decide whether to live for Jesus. But we don't just decide secretly, we pray and tell God how much we love him, and we also tell others."

Then the teacher might say, "Maybe you want to make the decision now. While we sing, 'Lord I want to be a Christian,' If you do, just kneel beside your chair and I'll come and pray with you."

Or, perhaps one teacher could go to another room with those who wish to pray, while the other teacher continues with the discussion. Even then, no pressure nor manipulative method is to be used. If, through realization of God's love in Christ, some respond in faith and commitment, we rejoice.

2. The decision should be an integral step in the child's growth.

While the conversion experience of the child is just as real as that of the adult, it is of necessity different. At no place does the harmfulness of trying to cram all persons into one type of religious experience become more obvious than here. In the child's experience there will not be so much emphasis on guilt and repentance as on salvation for useful and joyous living. If the conversion experience is a natural high point decision, integral to other church experiences, it is normal for the child to receive guidance in the Christian life-style from the church.

3. A person-to-person approach.

If parents are close to a child and keep the communication channels open, the child will usually come to them with feelings of need. There the parent calmly converses with the child, to help the child understand the meaning of the decision, and pray until a sense of being forgiven and being dedicated to Christ occurs.

Sometimes the parent will sense the need to open the conversation. As the child enters pre-adolescence doubts about self and the future may arise. The parent may open the conversation by his or her own witness. "You know, the thing that helps me most when I have trouble is prayer and my Christian faith. How do you feel about your relationship to God?" Or, just a simple question like "Do you feel you are a Christian?" may provide the opportunity for a depth decision, or for a growth experience.

4. Every teacher should be an evangelist.

The ultimate aim of all Christian teaching is that every pupil may have a personal relationship with God, through Jesus Christ, and that that relationship be an ever-deepening one. Some teachers are being evangelists by laying foundations of trust and love. To others come the privilege of confrontation and decision. Upon the teachers of juniors and early youth falls the greatest responsibility, for most definite decisions for Christ come between the ninth and twelfth years.

How may a teacher proceed in this very personal and life-changing opportunity?

(a) Develop a real friendship with each child. Even here deep concern and sensitivity is required, therefore the person-to-person approach seems most appropriate. Surely a teacher can build an experience of friendship and trust with each of ten or fifteen children. They will have done fun things together, as well as Bible study and service. They have discussed their problems, their values, and their life purposes. Perhaps the teacher has shared some of the more meaningful religious experiences as a child or youth.

(b) Make opportunities to be with groups of children. Some teachers invite children to their home or out for dinner. Some work together on a project. A camping trip may provide just the right atmosphere. Each teacher will find a way to talk to children about their relationship with God. Certainly such an experience must be intrinsic to the nature of the relationship. Perhaps we err more often on the side of not speaking than on the side of speaking too much.

(c) Share what Christ means to you. The teacher will need to be honest and specific. The teacher may tell about a personal conversion, or some recent hard decisions or of some other Christian's decision and life. Usually the child or youth will respond according to his or her own need. Sometimes the teacher may ask the child about life and a personal relationship to God. Sometimes there may be no response, then the teacher will not press, but change the subject and try to make their experience together a happy time.

One conversation went like this:

Teacher: Carolyn, I know you are a good student and very sincere in all you do. What do you want to be when you finish school?

Carolyn: Oh, I don't know but I want to help

poor people, so many kids don't have friends or anything.

Teacher: Are there some of these poor children in your school?

Carolyn: Yes, but the other kids laugh at them and I don't like that. But I don't help them either because then the kids would laugh at me.

Teacher: None of us like to be laughed at. Where do we get help to do what we think is right?

Carolyn: We could pray, but I don't think God would hear me because I just don't want kids to laugh at me.

Teacher: Don't you think God would understand how you feel and that you care about poor kids?

Carolyn: Well, yes, I guess so, but I know He would want me to be friends to them.

Teacher: How do you feel then about your Christian experience? Do you feel that you can pray about other things?

Carolyn: I don't know if I'm a Christian. When I was little I prayed and all that, but now I don't know.

Teacher: We all come to the time when we have to make this decision for ourselves.

Carolyn: I just did what my mother and teacher told me to do, and now I don't know whether I'm a Christian or not.

Teacher: Do you feel like you are ready to make the decision to be a Christian now that you are older?

Carolyn was in a church where a great deal of emphasis was put on the altar. She said she thought she ought to go to the altar. She went to the altar the next Sunday night. The teacher prayed with her and she made a definite decision. She has been a growing, serving Christian ever since.

With other children the decision and prayer would follow the personal conversation. Others might show no readiness for such a decision, and some may even say "no."

As Mary Alice Jones says, "There will come a time when there should be a definite explication of the Christian faith on the part of parents, teachers, and pastors, and a definite commitment to it on the part of boys and girls. There should be sharpened up for them the necessity of making a real choice for the direction of their lives: they should be helped to become aware of "the challenge of God' of the necessity of making decision between the will of God and their own will."[9]

Parents and teachers have the privilege of cooperating with God in interpreting the divine plan of salvation to children. They can witness to God's power and love in their own lives. They can show children how God can help them to overcome their own self will and free them to live a life of joyous fellowship with others Christians. They can present the choices and pray that each child will accept the salvation which God so freely offers.

(d) Give personal care and guidance. Another advantage of the person-to-person approach is the continuing relationship which makes guidance a natural part of the total experience. Children and youth need an understanding adult as counselor and sponsor. Such a person can interpret the child's experience to other adults and can help the new Christian over the rough spots of doubt and temptation. The adult counselor can encourage the child to fully participate in the ordinances of the church and can help the individual find opportunity for the expression of the Christian life through witness and service.

Conversation and nurture following decision-making is an essential and rewarding component of true evangelism.

CHAPTER V

Why Didn't They Speak?

He stood there like a naked self, crying for help. He had just learned that he was adopted and that his mother had never been married. His cry had become a defiant act against the church and even a denial of the personhood of Christ. He was hungry for love and meaning. He wanted to be forgiven, to regain a sense of worth to believe, but somehow he couldn't ask. The teacher heard the cry. She wanted to help him. She yearned for him to know Christ as a personal Savior. She wanted to say, "God loves you, such things don't matter to God." But she just said, "I'll hope to see you in my Sunday school class next Sunday." And they parted, two hungry people. Why didn't they speak?

They were two young people at camp. One had great doubts and had rebelled against the religion of her parents. She longed to become a Christian and invited her Christian friend for a walk on the pier at sunset. All day long she struggled with decision. All day long she hoped her friend would be aware of her hunger for Christ. So they went for a walk. They talked about the camp. They talked about their boyfriends—and the sunset and then—they came home. Why didn't they speak?

1. Evangelism must grow out of deep concern. "If I say, 'I will not mention him, or speak any more in his name' there is in my heart as it were a burning fire shut up in my bones, and I am weary with holding it in, and I cannot" (Jeremiah 20:9 RSV).

Evangelism will never be genuine until there is a "burning fire shut up within our bones that we cannot hold in." True, there is a relationship to be developed before words can have meaning. Yes, one must earn the right to talk to a person about the greatest decision he will ever make. We realize that. The winning of a soul is not to be programmed. Yet, there comes a time to speak to persons about Christ and their personal relationship with God.

2. The church should provide guidance in evangelism. Even though youth may have made an earlier decision for Christ, such a decision may need affirming now that they are no longer children. Often other youth who are spiritually alive are the best evangelists to youth. Christian education, therefore, will provide counsel and preparation so that Christian youth will carry concern for others and know how to help them to a genuine experience of conversion.

Such preparation would include at least the following elements:

(a) Learning how to open up a conversation. The teacher talking with the adopted boy might say, "Jerry, I notice that you seem to have some

39

problems about the church. Can you tell me how you feel?" Or she might say, "You seem to be having a hard struggle, if ever I can help you, I'm ready and willing." Or she might just frankly say, "I just learned that you found your mother this summer. I understand your struggle, but such things really do not matter to me or to God. God loves you and wants to help you to love Him."

The friend at the camp might say, "We've been talking about lots of things. Now let's talk about being Christian. I've been a Christian now for three years and I think it's the only life. How do you feel about being Christian?

(b) The biblical teachings and verses which make clear the meaning of conversion. The most effective introduction seems to be to show God's redeeming love as revealed in Christ Jesus. Such scriptures as John 3:16; Romans 5:8; 1 John 4:16, could be used. The natural response to a realization of God's love is to return love and to ask forgiveness. Again the Bible makes this clear and promises forgiveness. Suitable scriptures are: 1 John 4:19; 1 John 1:9; Acts 2:38. Faith is essential for the new Christian life. Scriptures on salvation through faith are: Gal. 2:20; Acts 16:31; Romans 3:27, 28. Then the continuing act is to commit himself to God in discipleship. Such scriptures as John 14:23, 24, 25 and John 15:12-17, make the commitment to follow Christ and his lifestyle clear.

(c) How to help another to Christ. If persons understand the clear teachings on a response to God's love in repentance, faith and commitment, surely they can lead another in prayer until the person responds to God's love, has faith that he or she has been accepted by God, and makes a commitment to follow the Christian way. There need not be a set pattern, only an authentic response to God's call, and a genuine commitment to follow the call.

(d) Where to refer the new Christian for further guidance. Of course, the person who won the other to Christ must be available for counsel and prayer. However, new converts can affirm their life in Christ through a public confession. They need the support of the community of faith. They will want to be baptized and to participate in the church. So it becomes necessary that they have a conference with the pastor, and take further steps toward their maturity as active Christians. Some churches have regular classes where the pastor can deal with problems which they face, and where they find support from each other.

Along with Bible study and dialogue about winning others, role plays have been used effectively both with youth and adults. Some possible role plays:

(1) Use the situation of the two young people at camp discussed under "Why didn't they speak?" After they have talked about usual things, have the Christian to ask the doubter why she has rebelled against religion. Then let

them take it from there. After about five minutes, stop their conversation and have the group analyze the procedure. You may have them try a different approach or another couple may try to deal with the situation.

(2) Have two youth on a boat ride. One has no church background and knows little about becoming a Christian. The other has recently been converted but has grown up in the church. He is eager to witness and jumps right in by saying "Chuck, I wonder why you are not a Christian." Chuck answers, "I think I'm as good as you are." Then let them take it.

(3) For adults take some of the crises situations of life, such as marriage, the birth of a child, a death in the family, and let the Christian use these as avenues to witness and confrontation.

3. The youth program should include opportunity for deep personal searching. Such experiences as fireside rap sessions, youth retreats, and overnight camps provide warm, close relationships that can become high points of decision if leaders direct the experience to depth dialogue. Given such a setting, leaders and youth with evangelistic concern, some religious singing, gospel or folk, Bible reading, prayer, and some searching questions, and who can predict what decisions will be made through the call of the Holy Spirit? It was just such an experience as this about which the following letter was written:

"Perhaps you don't remember that I was one

of the boys in your group at Camp Warner so long ago. I do want you to know, however, that I remember the sessions vividly and I do attribute many of my basic Christian concepts and convictions to times I spent in your classes. One thing that has stuck with me through the years is this: One time you said that if a person was faced with two choices and they were both Christian but one was a little more noble than the other, it was the duty of the Christian to do the most noble. This has been a guiding principle when I have been faced with a situation of that type.

"I know it is rather late but I do want to thank you most sincerely for the influence you had upon my life during its very impressionable years. Probably one of the reasons that I am so very happy today as a result of working in the ministry can be attributed to you and your influence those years ago."

4. Personal interviewing is a rich opportunity for evangelism. One youth minister explains the plan and response in the following paragraphs:

"As a youth minister, I have been frustrated by the fact that there were very few opportunities to have one-to-one relationships with youth in which I could help them explore their faith. I'd see them in the hall, classroom, recreation, and group worship experiences. However, it seemed that I rarely had the opportunity, the right environment, or a suitable amount of time at those events to ask that all important question, "How are things between you and God?"

"It was with that question in mind that I began to dream of a plan. I decided to ask each of the youth to come in for a personal interview just to get to know each other better. To have something to talk about, and to start a file on each of the youth, I drew up a questionnaire. It began with a list of single words such as: school, church, sex, Bible, marriage, marijuana, killing, and many more. On each of these I asked them to respond in one word or a phrase. The second part consisted of several questions dealing with people that had influenced their lives, what needed the most improvement in their lives, who can they talk to when they had a problem, and where they were in their Christian experience.

"Each youth spent about fifteen minutes in filling out the questionnaire and then about twenty minutes in one-to-one dialogue. I did not try to cover all the areas that they responded to, but asked them if there was a particular area or question that they wanted to talk about. After we spent time on what they wanted to talk about, I moved to, if we already had not, talking about a relationship with God.

"As we talked about their relationship with God, they expressed feelings of being lost, just starting out, being unsure of any relationship, really wanting to be a Christian but not knowing how, being at the bottom compared to most Christians, being nowhere, having a relationship that would not be accepted by the church, and many other expressions of deep feelings and convictions that prompted meaningful diagogue.

"Our dialogue about God was truly an experience of the Spirit. It provided us with an opportunity, not for me to simply evangelize, but to give witness to what I had experienced and to share in the experiences of the youth. I found that I was often humbled by the maturity of their faith. We found that we both had been asking the same questions that we thought we were alone in asking. As we struggled for answers, we experienced the Spirit of God growing inside. Many of the interviews ended in a prayer for God to help us both grow in his wisdom and understanding.

"As a direct result of these times together, I found many more opportunities for depth dialogue with the youth I had interviewed. We had developed a level of trust and understanding that is hard to obtain in a large group or in casual passing. I would not attempt to speak as to the total effectiveness of that interview on the youth, but to me the opportunity to witness and share was and is, a growing experience in the Spirit."

ADULTS NEED CHRIST, TOO

Each adult is unique. Each one makes an individual response to God's call. Adults cannot be regimented or put into a rigid formula. Yet all who testify to the Christian experience have one thing in common—they know that they have a new life in Christ and a new relationship with others.

Adults may have been deeply hurt. They may be indifferent or bitter, but in all there is a God-given hunger for this new life in Christ. How can we who care show them Christ as the answer to their hunger?

"Touched by a loving heart
Wakened by kindness
Chords that were broken
Will vibrate once more."

1. Christians must reach out. Adult Sunday school classes, if they are a dynamic fellowship and have a "burning fire shut up within their bones" can be a powerful agent of evangelism. Through such a group adults may reach out in friendship and love beyond the Christian circle. Most adults seem hungry for a meaningful relationship with a caring group. If they can feel themselves accepted in such a group, they are likely to respond in love to the group and to God, through Christ.

The class could also plan a strategy for helping members to relate to others who are not yet Christians. Some examples are:

(a) Coffee cup evangelism. The Christian invites a friend for coffee and shares his witness.

(b) Bible study evangelism. Neighbors get together for Bible study and invite non-Christians to attend.

(c) Quest or Koinonia groups. These are for depth relationships and spiritual renewal.

(d) Welcome evangelism. Relate on a one-to-one basis to new persons and families in the community. Show them friendship. Invite them into a Sunday school class, a quest group or Bible study group. Help them find a church.

(e) Prayer breakfasts. This method has been particularly effective with men.

(f) Helps evangelism. Provide transportation or various manual skills to people in need.

Each Christian will find a way to build friendships with non-Christians. If the relationship is genuine there will come a time when it is natural to speak about Christ. With adults some crises may open the door, just when the need is greatest.

2. Christians must take a stand against injustice and evil. Wherever the dignity of humanity is suffering at the hands of evil persons, let Christians espouse the cause of justice and right. Even though this may bring criticism and persecution, it can be humanity's loudest witness for Christ.

3. The church will provide services that reach new persons. The churches of one community recently visited every home and frankly asked the people what the churches could do to make their lives more meaningful. Out of the answers there developed an afternoon learning center and Bible study for children, a recreation program for youth, and a fellowship for senior adults.

The church day care center and the nursery school have been avenues of reaching young parents as well as the children. Some churches have classes for retarded children, some have religious libraries open after school. Others have a full program of camps and retreats. Whatever needs of people are not being met under suitable conditions, become the concern of the church.

Such services are the fruits of being Christian, and open doors for person-to-person dialogue about a personal relationship to God. In evangelism, too, there is the language of relationship and the language of words—there comes a time to speak!

4. The church will care for those who respond. Young Christians, of whatever age, need guidance and support in their new experience. They may be assured of their relationship with God, but there's a life pattern to be adopted. The church's practices may seem strange and lack meaning. Their friends and even their family may not understand. How can the church minister to them without taking over their very lives? I heard a missionary say that the church was his very mother and father. He had been orphaned at an early age, and the church had been his source of strength and finally led to his call to serve Christ abroad.

(a) Responsible persons in the church could become sponsors or big brothers or sisters to new Christians. This was true in the early Christian church. Paul thought of Timothy as his own son. Except for the love and determination of Barnabas, John Mark might have been lost.

I, myself, have known the strength that comes from such persons. As a child my Sunday school teacher first spoke to me about a definite decision for Christ. She went with me to the altar and prayed with me there. She often invited me to her home and opened up the opportunity for me to tell her my problems and to pray about them. She also mentioned my name as teacher for my first Sunday school class.

As a youth, the counselor was available for any problem or need. She gave a New Testament to every youth who graduated from our high school. She asked us if we were reading it. She took me with her when she visited the sick, and on one evangelistic tour. She helped me get a scholarship loan for college, and even signed the note.

As a young adult, I felt called to leave public school teaching and go into Christian education work, but there seemed no source of financial support. A sponsor believed in me and the cause enough to personally underwrite my salary for a year.

These are meanings of sponsor—a person who cares and has a watchful eye, one who believes in you and is willing to take risks to see that you have a chance to serve. What a rich relationship becomes possible for each partner!

(b) The church could have a sharing group for new converts. Usually such a group is led by the pastor and deals with questions and problems of the group. There guidance can be given in personal devotions, preparation for baptism, witnessing, and being Christian at school or at work. The group should be very informal, preferably meeting in a home. There should be free sharing, acceptance, and deep caring for one another. The group might become a more permanent quest or Bible study group.

(c) The church should help young converts find their place to work and witness. Young converts may not have great wisdom, but they have a fresh and radiant experience to share. No other experience will bring growth so quickly as sharing in the church's work. Perhaps they can be teamed with an experienced worker who might also act as a guide and sponsor. And so the process goes on—those who have been evangelized become evangelists. This is God's plan for the kingdom!

CHAPTER VI

A Responding People — The Church

"All my life I've been a traveler. One of the first things a traveler has to learn is to accommodate himself to the place and time in which he lives. He has to eat strange food, use an unfamiliar coinage, learn not to blush among people who have no privies, search for the good that subsists in the grossest and most primitive societies. Every individual, every organization has to sustain a conversation with the rest of the world. He cannot talk always in negatives and contradictions." I read this quote after a day of "accommodating" high up in the Andes in Cuzco, Peru. Along with the exiled priest, Jean Telemond as given in West's novel *The Shoes of the Fisherman,* all who have traveled know that the first part of the quote is true. But at present we are more concerned about the last part of the quote. "Every individual, every organization has to sustain a conversation with the rest of the world." He continues to say, "They (speaking of the people in today's world) grapple every day with every human dilemma, from birth to death, but they hear no trumpets, see no Crusader's cross lifted up."[10]

Rejoice! The church is now beginning to blow the trumpets and lift the Crusader's cross high. Catapulted out of its dullness by criticism, threat and suffering the church seems to be emerging into a period of joy and victory.

Such victory, coupled with a love and deep concern for winning people to the Christian way was a mark of the early church.

Jesus' sermon as recorded in John 15 speaks of obedience, love, and joy. "If you obey my commands, you will remain in my love . . . I have told you this that your joy may be complete. This is my commandment: love one another, just as I love you." (John 15:10-12 TEV).

The today folk version may be "Joy is like the Rain" or "They'll know we are Christian by Our Love," but this is another attempt to express the same spirit as that of the early church.

HOW DOES THE CHURCH WITNESS TODAY?

1. The church witnesses through the quality of its own life. We cannot think of Christian education as evangelism outside of the context of the church as a community of love. R. Eugene Sterner has helped us to realize this in his book, *Being the Community of Christian Love.* He holds that the sickness of this day is alienation. He says alienation is three pronged: "The sense of separation from the righteous

God, frustration and confusion within oneself, hostility against other people and the cruel impersonal forces found in society."[11] Then he gives the church as the place where a person may find himself or herself by becoming a part of a redemptive group. People are hungry to be a part of a redemptive, supportive fellowship with Christ at the center. As Elton Trueblood said, "The creation of such a fellowship is the argument that can count in the confused world of our day. . . . If there should emerge in our day such a fellowship, wholly without artificiality and free from the dead hand of the past, it would be an exciting event of momentous importance. A Society of loving souls set free from self-seeking struggle for personal prestige and from all unreality would be something unutterably precious."[12]

The key word in such a group is "servanthood." Our greatest witness is our deepest relationship.

The well-known theologian, Martin Buber, held that all meaning in life is based on a meeting, but that there are two distinct kinds of meeting. . . . There is an I-Thou meeting and an I-It meeting. When a Christian treats another as a "thou," that means acceptance as a person worthy of respect, even though the person may be living far from the Christian way. The Christian tries to understand how life looks and to hear the real need. If the witness can be one of honest personal concern and real listening, it may become an I-Thou meeting in which the Eternal-Thou will be the chief participant. Such is a church evangelistically alive.[13]

2. The church witnesses through its message. The church's message in teaching, in preaching, and in personal witness is clear "For God loved the world so much that he gave his only Son, so that everyone who believes in him may not die but have eternal life" (John 3:16 TEV). All evangelism must set forth realistically the reality of sin, the power of God's love and grace for the forgiveness of sin and for the transformation of life. There is no pat formula by which one responds to this message. There are varieties of Christian response, and each person is unique. If as Georgia Harkness says, we could see the church for what it is—"a fallible human instrument but with a divine commission for carrying out Christ's work in the world," we could witness with more courage. "The church exists to be the carrier of the gospel of Christ to the inner lives of [people] and to the world."[14]

3. The church's witness is to the whole person.

I met with a group of world Christians in Peru in the summer of 1971. Our purpose was to study conditions in order to find a more effective way to bring the message of Christ to the world and especially to Latin America. One morning the group found a handwritten letter tacked to the wall. In part it read:

"As searchers for human dignity we welcome you to one of the most repressive states in the world today, with the hope that the Christian message of freedom and liberation may be heard. But we share with the poor and oppressed a silent grin at your naive intentions.

"We have met many people passing through our country with good intentions, who were unwilling to commit themselves to our liberation. We are skeptical of the church's sincerity and your stated concern for our lives.

"We challenge you to re-examine your Christian commitment to include not only "all men" but also "all the man" in his political, social, and economic life so that freedom and justice might be ours and yours."

The church is called to witness to the love of God to all people. This includes those with whom we live and work as well as all persons in the far parts of the earth. But the Latin student was right when he said the call is a commitment to bring justice and liberation to humanity in all areas of life. The Bible is clear on this subject too. One has only to be sensitive to the ministry of Jesus, or to read the book of James to know that faith and works are interwoven in a whole gospel. The witness to God's love can never be as strong as when it is accompanied by commitment to justice for all humankind.

THE CHURCH AS A
RESPONDING PEOPLE

Each human being is called to place a personal stamp upon the world. Whether it be in a classroom, in home, in office, shop, factory, on the farm, in legislative hall, or on some bed of helplessness and suffering—each one of us is saying something to the world.

"And what we are saying to the world is being heard by others—It is not always for us to determine in what setting we shall speak, but it is for us to have a voice in determining what our lives will say."[15]

We are the church—a responding people. All Christians are called to respond: "yield themselves to the Holy Spirit, live in obedience to the will of God in every relationship and fulfill their common discipleship and mission in the world."

Each person who would be a disciple of Christ does well to ask: Do I truly think of life as a calling to win others to the abundant life? Do I see myself as a servant, called into the redeeming, healing, saving ministry of God in the world? How will my "yes" to life and to God find its most meaningful expression?

Bibliography

1 Wayne E. Oates, *On Becoming Children of God.* Copyright MCMLXIX, Westminster Press,—Phila.—1969, p. 15. Used by permission.*

2 Gordon Allport, *Becoming.* Yale University Press, 1955, pp. 94-98.

3 Sherrill, Lewis J., *The Struggle of the Soul.* Macmillan, N.Y., 1963, paperback, p. 190. Copyright 1951 by Lewis J. Sherrill.

4 Hoffman, Adeline M., Ph.D., *The Daily Needs and Interests of Older People.* Charles C. Thomas, Springfield, IL, 1970, p. 185.

5 Ibid.

6 Potthoff, Harvey H., *The Inner Life.* Graded Press, Nashville, 1969, p. 184. Used by permission.

7 Elisabeth C. Hewitt from *Hymnal of the Church of God.* Warner Press, 1971, p. 326.

8 By Harold Johnson in *Basics for Teaching in the Church,* Miller, T. Franklin; Welton, Beverly; Miller, James Blair; Johnson, Harold; Hall, Kenneth F., Copyright 1968 by T. Franklin Miller, Warner Press, p. 115. Used by permission.

9 Jones, Mary Alice, *The Faith of our Children.* Copyright 1943 by Whitmore and Stone. Used by permission of Abingdon Press.*

10 Morris L. West, *The Shoes of the Fisher-*

man. Deli Pub. Co., N.Y., p. 211. Copyright 1963 by Morris L. West. Used by permission of William Morrow and Co. Inc.*

11 Sterner, R. Eugene, *Being the Community of Christian Love*. Copyright 1971, Warner Press, Inc. p. 14. Used by permission.

12 Trueblood, Elton, *Alternative to Futility*. Harper and Row Publishers, Inc. p. 34. Used by permission.

13 Buber, Martin, *I and Thou*. Trans. Ronald G. Smith (Scribner), 1958.

14 Harkness, Georgia, *The Ministry of Reconciliation*. Abingdon Press, p. 75. Used by permission.*

15 Potthoff, Harvey H., *The Inner Life*. Graded Press, Nashville, p. 186. Used by permission.

16 (Pages 24, 28, 55, 57—From The Today's Version of The New Testament. Copyright American Bible Society, 1966.

*out of print

A Guide for the Effective Use of "The Teacher As Evangelist"

Many Runways . . . Find the Right Approach!

Preliminary discussions for this guide were held in the terminal building of the St. Louis Lambert International Airport. Watching the planes land and take off provided an analogy of the educational evangelistic task of the church. There are many runways from which a plane can take off but the important thing is to find the right approach when you consider wind velocity, air traffic, and other vital factors. Many plans of evangelism have been developed over the last few years, each being very valuable in its own way. Our concern is that you discover the "right approach" for your own ministry.

The material in this book can be used in a variety of ways. Begin by evaluating the evangelism of your own church. Proceed, then, to use this material to produce maximum benefits in your program. Caution should be exercised in simply using a plan out of a book. Let the material become so much a part of you and your church that it has particular meaning and value to all persons in your church. Try to envision the persons you desire to see respond to salvation, this will help the approach you develop for your class or department.

Evangelism Does Not Just Blossom Overnight

Jesus requested the disciples to "wait" until they were filled with the Holy Spirit and then they were to be witnesses (Acts 1:4-8). The waiting does not make the time element indispensable but it does imply that witnessing requires something more than just a desire to lead persons to Christ. For that reason many churches will want to use the pamphlet for a series of six "evangelism exploration" sessions in which you pray, study and seek God's will for your witnessing program through the Sunday church school. These sessions could be geared to six consecutive evening teacher-training periods or used in special focus meetings with your staff.

PLAN 1—Six Sessions in Outline

Session I: Exploring Evangelism and Education
  A. Biblical basis . . . is steadfast.
  B. Evangelism: Instantaneous and Progressive.

  Basic Reading—Chapter I

  Additional Resources: *Effective Evangelism,* by George Sweazy; *Master Plan of Evangelism,* by Robert Coleman; and *Evangelism Explosion,* by James Kennedy.

Explore together the relationship between evangelism and education in the church.

Session II: The Growing Grain! (John 4:35)
  A. From birth to bud! (0 to 5)
  B. From bud to blossom! (Grade 1 to teens)
  Basic Reading—Chapter II

Additional Resources: *Toward Effective Teaching* series—*Young Children, Elementary Children, Youth; Struggle of the Soul,* by Lewis J. Sherrill.

Discuss thoroughly the development of the growing child in the church school. Possible interview with one of today's teen-agers.

Session III: The Ripened Years! (Joel 3:13)
  A. Today's Young Adult . . . quest for identity.
  B. Middle Adult . . . quest for reality.
  C. Older Adult . . . quest for dignity and destiny.

  Basic Reading—Chapter III

  Additional Resources: *Toward Effective Teaching—Adults,* by Norman Jacobs; *One Way to Win the World,* by Leighton Ford.

Discuss modern means of reaching the ripened spiritual harvest in today's adult world. Why are we not communicating the "good news" to them? How can we change to become more effective in witnessing to them?

Session IV: Harvest Time! (Matthew 9:37-38)
  A. Awareness of the worker . . . we are to win men to Christ.
  B. The heart of the goal of Christian education is to bring the pupil to a definite decision for Christ.
  C. Relationship prepares the way through which the Holy Spirit produces the conversion.

  Basic Reading—Chapter IV

Additional Resources: *Teacher, You Are an Evangelist* by Mary Latham; *The Secret of Soul Winning,* by Stephen Olford.

Explore opportunities for building relationship with pupils and moving from that to a definite decision for Christ.

Session V: "Sow in Tears . . . Reap in Joy" (Psalm 126:5-6)

    A. Compassion, motivation for witnessing.

    B. Equipping the workers, types of approach:
        Coral Ridge Plan . . . James Kennedy
        Four Spiritual Laws . . . Bill Bright
        Peace With God . . . Billy Graham
        Roman Road . . . Gospel in Romans
        Search for other techniques of this nature
        and share with the persons in your group.

Basic Reading—Chapter V

Additional Resources: *Saturation Evangelism,* by George W. Peters; *Evangelism Now,* compilation from the U.S. Congress on Evangelism; *Evangelism in the Home Church,* by Andrew W. Blackwood, *On the Grow,* by Charles Shumate.

Discuss and evaluate various types of soul winning techniques. Do they agree with New Testament theology? What are the weaknesses of such programs, if any? Do they minister to the "whole" man or are there blind spots to consider? List at least 12 ways of sharing your faith with others.

Session VI: Education + Evangelism = Response!

    A. First response . . . love for Christ and the church.

B. Response through ... speaking out ... for Christ.

C. Response through ... reaching out ... for others.

Basic Reading—Chapter VI

Additional Resources: *New Testament Follow-Up for Pastors and Laymen,* by Waylan B. Moore; *Jesus and the Disinherited,* by Howard Thurman; *Where Are You Going, Jesus?* by R. Eugene Sterner; *A Place to Stand,* by Elton Trueblood.

Discuss: Can a Christian produce lasting fruits of social redemption without first having the roots of righteousness? Speaking the truth is the responsibility of the Christian ... can we truly be evangelistic unless we speak directly to the great issues of this day? Can we be an evangelistic church and seek only to "save" the soul while the person suffers in the world? Is our soul winning the type of evangelism that really loves, accepts and understands the person different from ourselves?

PLAN II: Six Hours of Intensive Training

Knowing something of the pressures of the day it will be necessary for some congregations to have this study in a more intensive type of training. To do this you could take the outline for the six separate days and use it in six one-hour periods of study. It will be impossible to digest the material unless you make some outside reading assignments at least two weeks in advance. This approach could be presented with a time of preparation of outlined reading, then meet together for three consecutive nights of two hours each. An alternate plan would include a Friday night for two hours, followed by four hours of study on Saturday, breaking at noon for lunch. Be creative in taking the basic guidelines and develop the training program that will relate best to your church schedule and needs. If possible, one might use a retreat setting in which you study together, ending with a period of renewed commitment to Christ on the part of the individual teachers.

PLAN III: Ministers' Meeting

District or sectional ministers' meetings could make good use of the book as the basis for conferences on education and evangelism. Invite one of the associate secretaries from the national Board of Christian Education to provide leadership as you explore this opportunity in outreach and ministry. In such a training session the pastor could be equipped to return home and lead his church school staff in the study of the material. Ministers' meetings provide the atmosphere for wrestling with some of the important concerns that surround both education and evangelism.

PLAN IV: Issue Oriented Approach

Issues intensify our interest in education/evangelism. Within the book one can identify some vital issues confronting the church as we seek to evangelize the world. Valuable "in-depth discussion" can be held by small groups wrestling with the issues.

Issue 1: *What is vital in our church's ministry?*

In a day of disenchantment with the organized church, is there a valid reason for our existence as a movement? What ministry is the church now performing that she could cease doing without failing in her task? Could the church continue her ministry without the Scripture? Could she continue without evangelism? How vital is evangelism and education to the church?

Issue 2: *Significant changes are constantly taking place in the growing child. List the changes taking place at each level mentioned in the book. How do these relate to the possible conversion of the child?*

In what way do you communicate your faith to the infant child? What changes are taking place in the kindergarten child to help in understanding God's love? Does hypocrisy in the church affect the primary or middler child? Hero worship is a part of the pre-adolescent, does this say anything to the person working with these children? How would you explain the "plan of salvation" to this age level? Try to remember the changes taking place in your life as a teenager. In what way did that affect your decision for Christ?

Issue 3: *Identity the basic issues confronting the individual at each stage of adult life.*

Has the church made the gospel relevant to the young adult? In our preaching/teaching have we helped childhood faith mature as the adult ages chronologically? With the foundation of the family being shaken by societal and moral changes, how does the church win the middle adult to Christ? Many older adults find life void of meaning and therefore feel useless. In seeking to win them to Christ do we bring them to a meaningful, useful existence? Or do we simply see them saved and leave them as lonely, useless and frustrated as before?

Issue 4: *What determines a definite decision or conversion?*

Should teachers be recruited on the basis of how many they have led to Christ? Do you provide training for teachers, giving them guidance in how to teach for decision? Do your teachers visit in the pupil's home, making possible a "person to person" soul winning approach? As a teacher, do you believe that you were really called to be an evangelist?

Issue 5: *In this day of great opportunity how has your church met the challenge to share her faith?*

What do you understand the term "soul burden" to mean? Is it more than just a surface concern for the unsaved? What training does your church provide in this area of evangelism? How can we make better use of the opportunities our church school curriculum provides to help pupils make a decision for Christ? How can the church equip teachers to be soul winners? What kind of soul winning material do you presently use? Is the material theologically sound? Does it minister to the total person? Do you believe that when the church is witnessing through servanthood that evangelism is being carried out even though there are no definite decisions recorded?

Issue 6: *What needs of people is your congregation's ministry designed to meet?*

Basically, people need to be saved from sin but does our "seeking to save" end there? Read Matthew 25:31-46, and James 2 then discuss this issue in the light of these passages. Compare also the words of Jesus as recorded in Luke 4:18. In ministering to the "total" person, what part does the worship and preaching play in this evangelism? What can we do to make our congregations more "redemptive" to those whom we have won to Christ? In many soul winning programs the converts are never established in the local church ... does God hold us accountable for helping them to "grow in grace and knowledge of the Lord and Savior, Jesus Christ?" What plans for "soul conservation" have you established in your local church? Do you presently have a ministry to help persons who are poverty striken, blind, deaf, imprisoned or of another race? Do you see this as being related to evangelism/education?

PLAN V: Additional Options

Great benefits are available for the leader who selects certain areas of the book to be explored in depth by selected, interested persons. To make the learning experience more enjoyable, the following options are suggested for possible use as you involve your people in education and evangelism.

1. *Role Playing* is always an effective means of communication. It would be helpful to use this with the suggestions made on pages 34-35 of the book. Any small group can use this since it is simply the "impromptu acting out of a situation or incident, enabling groups or individuals to identify with other groups or individuals." Let someone project himself or herself into these situations, acting out how he or she really feels in certain circumstances. The actor in the role play will try to understand how the other person should respond to these methods of witnessing or soul winning. Remember, your role playing involves imagination and response without a script, attempting to sense what the other person feels. Be creative in trying to find many ways of opening up a conversation that will lead to a definite decision in the conversion of the unsaved. Do not fail though to give specific directions as to who plays certain roles and what is the real purpose of this approach. Four situations to consider: Openers at the door when canvassing a neighborhood for new

families; a presentation of the gospel in someone's home and their response; leading a person in your class to make a definite decision; presenting the gospel in your office, your automobile, a plane, or business situation.

2. *In-Service Training Produces Results.* This plan would involve both classroom instruction and field service. Use the book as study material for the foundation of the program and then let the lesson become experiential as you teach the class, visit in the home, serve in a retreat, or deal on a person-to-person basis. The program is built upon the premise that the worker learns more when he begins to apply what you have been studying in the book. Following each weekly training session and field experience let the persons involved join together in a time of evaluating their witness. What were your strong points? Were you sensitive to the other person's need and reactions? What were your weak points? In what areas do you need special assistance? If possible it would be good to enroll the entire staff of teachers in this program so that your church school would understand the educational and evangelistic concept.

3. *Pastor to People interest development is a possibility.* Using the trainer/trainee approach, let the pastor first get thoroughly acquainted with the book, making full use of each section in his or her own personal

ministry. One cannot teach that which has not been tested in witnessing. Without the practical testing the pastor will only be sharing someone else's theory of education and evangelism. After having used the ideas of the book, outline the material for the number of times you will be sharing with the trainee. The trainee should be hand-picked by the pastor, giving special attention to selecting the person who is sensitive to the needs of others and is desirous of learning how to share one's faith in the educational ministry of the church. This could be a teacher, department head, assistant teacher or someone who would make a good church worker. Give attention to structuring the program over a given period of time so that the person being trained will know when the training begins and when it will end. Here again the trainer/traineee will meet each week, study together, pray together, serve together and then evaluate what they are doing to really achieve the main purpose, that of leading persons to Christ.

4. *Teacher Enlistment Requirement enables the Board of Christian Education to use this book with all church school workers for the new church school year.* If the teacher is an evangelist and we expect the teacher to teach for a definite decision, then the study of the book should be a requirement. Therefore, let the Board provide opportunities for the new staff to

study "The Teacher As Evangelist," purchasing each person their own copy, providing training in its use and then helping them to adapt its techniques in their area of service. It is only fair to the worker, if we expect that person to win people to Christ, that we provide not only the material but also the training in its effective use.

Some Biblical Resources

Historically, those churches that have experienced real growth have been based upon the Bible. For that reason it would appear wise if we are to educate and evangelize the world that we must use the scripture at every level possible in this study. Most scripture selection will be left to the discretion of the teacher, selecting that which will be most helpful in the situation in your church. Let us remember that scripture is used for more than proof for a particular theological position. Scripture reveals God's plan for redemption from sin and is the key to abundant life.

Some texts are listed here for the benefit of those counseling or seeking to lead someone to conversion in Christ.

All have sinned	God's part in our redemption	
Romans 3:23	Romans 5:8	Revelation 3:20
Romans 5:12	Luke 19:10	John 1:12
Isaiah 53:6	2 Peter 3:9	John 6:37

The penalty of sin	Our part in salvation
Romans 6:23	1 John 1:9
John 8:24	Romans 10:9
Hebrews 9:27	Romans 10:12-13
Ezekiel 18:21-23	Isaiah 55:6-7

What must I do to be saved?
   Acts 2:38-39.
   Acts 9:6

The Church . . . An Arena For Action!

Evangelism should be the natural outreach of the church. Christian education eventuates in developing soul winners. This, however, cannot be isolated to a narrow concept of evangelism . . . it must be based on the inclusiveness of the gospel, Christian education should open doors of understanding so that we will win persons to Christ at every "crossing point in human experience. In the context of the church there should be an atmosphere that is conducive to persons being born into the "family of God." Love should be the prevailing attitude and this leaves no room for discrimination, pride or bigotry.

Therefore, let the study include an enlargement of the last section of the book. Include such questions as these:

   a) How are we winning people to Christ?
   b) Are we concerned about all people (all races all ages, all types)?
   c) What continuing ministry do we have to the new converts?
   d) Do we openly accept war protestors? drug addicts? How do you relate to them?
   e) What are we doing to help . . . and to win . . . those in poverty?
   f) Are we concerned about the aged, particularly those confined to nursing homes?